11 September 2001 11 September 2001 11 September 2001 11 September 2001 11 September 2001 11 September 2001 11 September 2001 11 September 2001 11 September 2001 11 September 2001 11 September 2001 11 September 2001 11 September 2001 11 September 2001 11 September 2001 11 September 2001 11 September 2001 11 September 2001

Attack
on
America

11 September 2001

Attack
on
America

Brian Williams

CHERRYTREE
BOOKS

A Cherrytree Book

First published 2003
by Cherrytree Books
Evans Brothers Limited
2a Portman Mansions
Chiltern Street
London WIU 6NR

VISIT OUR WEBSITE
www.evansbooks.co.uk

First published in 2003

British Library Cataloguing in Publication Data

Williams, Brian,
    Attack on America. - (Dates with history)
    1. September 11 Terrorist Attacks, 2001 - Juvenile
    literature 2. United States - History - 1969 -
    I. Title
    973.9'31

ISBN 1842342029

Series Editor: Louise John
Editor: Mary-Jane Wilkins
Designer: Mark Holt
Maps: Tim Smith

Picture credits:
Associated Press AP: 14, 16, 18, 20, 22, 23, 24, 25, 26, 27,
    29, 31, 35, 36, 37, 38
Aviation Images: 12
Rex Features Limited: front cover, 11, 15, 17, 19, 21, 28,
    30, 32, 34, 39

Contents

A day like any other

Across the United States, 11 September 2001 began like any other day. The weather was clear and sunny. In New York City and Washington DC, thousands of people were on their way to work. Breakfast TV and the morning papers carried the usual world news. The Middle East **peace process** was going nowhere. There were more **terrorist** attacks. George Bush, President of the United States, was visiting a school in Florida.

New York City's two biggest buildings, the two World Trade Center towers, were coming to life. Every day 50,000 people came to work in the towers, which had 110 floors and stood 411 metres high.

The twin towers of the World Trade Center loomed over the other buildings in lower Manhattan before 11 September 2001.

A date no American will forget

The Pentagon in Washington is the heart of the US Department of Defense, and on the morning of 11 September it was humming with activity as usual.

At US airports, early flights were getting ready for take-off. At Boston's Logan Airport at 7.59 am **Eastern Time**, American Airlines Flight 11 took off for Los Angeles with 92 people on board.

Every day hundreds of passenger planes, like this American Airlines jet, are in the skies above the United States.

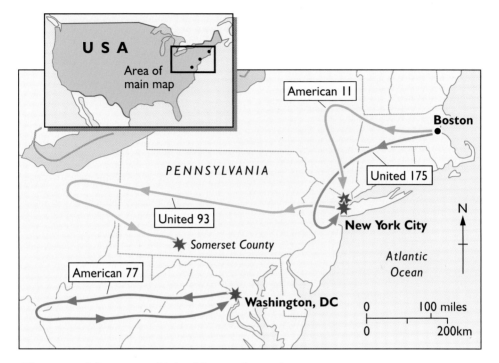

This map of the eastern United States shows the routes flown by the hijacked planes on 11 September.

At 8.14 am United Airlines Flight 175 left the same airport, also heading for Los Angeles.

Washington Dulles Airport was becoming busy too. American Airlines Flight 77 took off at 8.20 am. It too was flying west, to Los Angeles. The planes were less than half full at this early hour, and the passengers settled down for a routine trip.

Another day was beginning in the usual way, but 11 September was about to become a date that no American will forget.

13

The horror begins

At 8.42 am United Airlines Flight 93 left Newark, New Jersey. It was a Boeing 757, bound for San Francisco. As the plane climbed, the 46 passengers could see the familiar landscape below. There was New York City, with its **skyscraper** landmarks, topped by the World Trade Center's twin towers.

Smoke and flames pour out of the North Tower just after it was hit.

Inside those towers were the offices of 1,200 firms, with 50,000 **employees** from 60 different countries. Many workers were already at their desks, snatching time to gaze out of the window. Just before 8.45 am people in the North Tower saw a Boeing 767. It was coming much closer than normal, and was near enough for people to see its American Airlines markings. This was Flight 11 from Boston. As people watched in horror, the aircraft flew directly into the upper floors of the building and exploded in a mass of orange flame.

At first everyone thought that a terrible accident had happened. People began to **evacuate** the buildings, hurrying down the stairs to the street far below. Omar Rivera, who was blind, came down 71 floors guided by a friend, Donna Enright, and his guide dog Salty. Many people made hurried calls on their mobile phones. Firefighters from the Fire Department of New York raced to the tower, from which thick black smoke and flames were now billowing.

Firefighters fought their way through thick smoke and dust as they tried to rescue people from the burning building.

'This looks really bad'

People could not take in what had happened. The plane had exploded on hitting the North Tower. Its tanks were full of **jet fuel**, which burned fiercely. The airliner had become a giant firebomb, and had set fire to the building. Many people were trapped at the top of the North Tower above the flames. Many more below were scrambling to get out.

The television pictures looked unreal, like scenes from a disaster film. All over America, and in Europe (where it was now lunchtime), TV **newscasters** were trying to explain the events, without knowing what had happened. Then at 9.03 am, a second plane flew into the picture. It made a turn and flew straight towards the South Tower.

The second plane approaches the South Tower, while the North Tower burns fiercely.

The plane smashed into the South Tower, causing a huge explosion. This plane was United Airlines Flight 175, which had left Boston 49 minutes earlier.

Some of those trapped in the North Tower had time to make phone calls. Edmund McNally told his wife she'd have to cancel a surprise trip to Rome that he had booked; he did not think he would come out alive.

Two planes could not collide with a skyscraper by accident. Could this be a terrorist attack? From the 92nd floor of the burning South Tower, Tom McGinnis phoned his wife. 'This looks really, really bad,' he said. He told her he could see people falling from the floors above him.

Flight 175 explodes on impact with the South Tower, sending a fireball through the building.

17

Is this war?

In Sarasota, Florida, President Bush was reading to children in a classroom at the Emma E Booker elementary school. Andrew Card, his **chief of staff**, whispered an urgent message. The president looked stunned. He had been told the news from New York.

America's biggest city had been attacked without warning. Thousands of people might be dead. Was America at war? At 9.40 am a third plane (American Airlines Flight 77) roared in low across Washington, DC. It flew into the west side of the giant Pentagon building at 560 kph (350 mph).

The Pentagon is a five-sided building, which is
the command centre for US military forces.

Smoke pours from the side of the Pentagon, after Flight 77 had smashed a hole in the building.

The Pentagon has office space for 25,000 people. Many escaped alive, but 125 were killed as the plane struck. All 64 people on Flight 77 died. Many offices in the Pentagon were empty for rebuilding. Floors and windows had been strengthened. A new **sprinkler system** doused fires started by the crashed plane. Two hundred construction workers helped to carry out the wounded and guide 2,000 employees from their wrecked offices.

Air Force jets streaked across the skies, watching for more attacks. The Federal Aviation Authority ordered all non-military aircraft to stay on the ground. The **State Department** and part of the **White House** were hurriedly evacuated. The President set off to Washington by plane. For a time, no one really knew what was happening. Who was America's new and unseen enemy?

Collapse and rescue

The twin towers of the World Trade Center were now blazing beacons in a blue sky. The massive structures were constructed from steel tubes which were designed to be strong enough to stand up to fires, hurricanes or an earthquake. They stayed intact long enough for thousands of people to escape. The fires started by the crashing planes were so hot (around 1000°C) that the steel began to soften and bend.

The South Tower collapses while smoke continues to pour from the North Tower.

Although thousands had escaped, many more were trapped with no hope of rescue. At around 10 am, the South Tower collapsed. The giant building sank into itself, as the upper floors plunged through the floors below. Firefighters, police officers and other rescuers were buried under thousands of tonnes of rubble. Smoke and dust clouds rolled down

New York's streets, and ash fell like a blizzard of snow.
People ran into doorways or scrambled under cars
for shelter. Some recorded the horrific sight on video.

At 10.28 am the North Tower collapsed. It too sank
to earth, amid billowing clouds of smoke and dust which
choked the streets, and the rescuers below. Beneath the
mass of twisted metal and concrete were the remains of
more than 2,500 people. Among those killed were
people who had run into the buildings to help: 343 New
York firefighters and 60 police officers from the New
York police department and port authority. One
firefighter said later, *'It looked like an atom bomb hit it.'*

Firefighters with breathing equipment outside the twin towers.
Rescuers were covered in dust and ash when the towers collapsed.

The Capitol in Washington, DC, houses the Senate and the House of Representatives. It was a likely target of the fourth suicide attack. Another was the president's weekend home, Camp David.

and learned what had happened in New York City. They guessed that their plane too had become a flying bomb. In its path lay the nation's centre of government. The passengers had little doubt as to their fate.

A phone operator on the ground was talking to one of the passengers, Todd Beamer. He and some other passengers bravely decided to storm the pilots' cabin. *'Are you guys ready? Let's roll!'* he yelled. Over the phone came shouts and crashes. Then there was silence.

The pilots were probably already dead, killed by the hijackers who were now flying the plane. There must have been a violent fight between passengers and hijackers. The plane zigzagged out of control and crashed into a field near the town of Shanksville, Pennsylvania.

The world rallies behind America

The US **Secretary of State**, Colin Powell, was visiting Peru, and was having breakfast with Peru's president when he was told the news. 'Get the plane, we're leaving,' ordered the former army general. President Bush and his team gathered in Washington and began to plan America's response. Phone lines were jammed with calls to and from world leaders. The US armed forces were on full alert.

President Bush spoke to the American people from the White House that evening.

New York mayor Rudolph Giuliani spoke to reporters from a makeshift control centre. His emergency office in the World Trade Center had been completely destroyed, and City Hall was considered unsafe.

President Bush spoke to the American people on television. He called for a campaign against international terror. The **NATO** alliance declared that an attack on one member-country (the USA) was an attack on all 19 member-countries. Fire crews and rescue trucks were pouring into New York City, heading for the disaster site. Hospitals prepared to treat wounded casualties, but few were brought in.

Rescue dogs sniffed through the rubble, but they found no survivors. The streets were littered with odd shoes, hats, bags, torn clothing, fragments of office furniture and shattered computers.

At 5.25 pm a third building, 7 World Trade Center, also collapsed. Other buildings nearby were badly damaged and had to be made safe. No one knew how many people were dead.

Rescuers search the rubble in front of the shell of one of the twin towers.

Miraculous escapes

This was not the first attack on the World Trade Center. In 1993, 50,000 people had been evacuated after a **truck-bomb** exploded in the underground car park. On 9/11 (which is how Americans write 11 September), the twin towers were not so full because it was early in the day. Few tourists were around. The rescue services moved fast to get people out.

People ran for safety as the twin towers fell, one after the other.

Many people escaped by running down the stairs. The elevators stopped working after the planes hit the towers. Those who left their desks at once had the best chance.

Many were not so lucky. They stayed in their offices. People working above the explosion zone were unable to get down to ground level. Trapped by the flames, some people jumped from the upper floors to their deaths.

There were remarkable escape stories. Five men were trapped on their way up to the 70th floor of the North Tower when the elevator stopped, shook, fell and then stopped again. After ten minutes, a crackly voice on the intercom told them that the building had been hit. Smoke started pouring in. They forced open the doors and saw a wall on the 50th floor.

Window cleaner Jan Demczur slid the rubber off his **squeegee** and the men used the metal blade to hack a hole in the wall. They came to tiles, punched another hole and crawled through into a bathroom, to be greeted by startled firefighters. It took them an hour to walk down the fire escape. At 10.23 am they reached the street. At 10.28 the North Tower fell.

Ambulances from all over New York and the surrounding area came to transport the injured to hospital.

Clearing up

Hundreds of rescuers raced to the disaster sites on 9/11. During the first desperate day, firefighters and rescue teams worked for 20 hours at a stretch, with only snatched breaks for rest. The work went on under glaring floodlights at night, as rescuers clambered over the smouldering pile of rubble where the twin towers had stood – the site now named Ground Zero.

There were very few people to rescue. At midnight, two men were found trapped in an air pocket. One had to have a leg **amputated** before he could be pulled free. Five firefighters were pulled out alive at 5 am.

Rescue operations continued far into the night under powerful floodlights.

The streets around the World Trade Center looked like a battlefield. Mayor Giuliani called it 'the most horrific sight I've ever seen in my whole life.' He was working from a temporary office in a fire station, where the phones still worked.

The names and photos of missing people were posted in the streets as relatives and friends came for news of them. Restaurants put up tables on the sidewalks. People helped one another. A few criminals helped themselves; crime in New York rose after 9/11, as the police turned their attention to terrorism rather than burglary. At Ground Zero, there was a gaping hole in the New York skyline, where the twin towers had once risen high above the city.

People put up posters with the names and photos of missing friends or family members.

Hunting the hijackers

The US security agencies, including the **FBI**, began the hunt for the 9/11 terrorists. They first had to identify the hijackers, who were all dead. Piecing together vital scraps of information, the FBI named 19 men as the hijackers. Some held pilots' licences. Several had been living in the United States.

Mohammed Atta was named as a leader of the hijackers. He was on the plane which flew into the North Tower.

Detectives already had a theory about who had planned the hijacks. In the previous attack on the World Trade Center, in 1993, a bomb had been planted by terrorists belonging to al-Qaeda. Al-Qaeda was also thought to have bombed US **embassies** in Africa in 1998.

The al-Qaeda organisation was more secretive than other groups known to be active in the Middle East, such as Islamic Jihad (which had murdered Egypt's leader,

Anwar Sadat, in 1981) or Hamas and Hizbollah,
two Arab organisations fighting against Israel.

On 14 September 2001, the US government named
Osama bin Laden as the chief suspect. He was born
in Saudi Arabia in 1957, and was the 17th son of a
wealthy construction engineer. Bin Laden had had a
university education, but at the age of 22 had joined
Muslim fighters in Afghanistan. Later, he had turned
to terrorism. He was the leader of al-Qaeda, and had
recruited people willing to carry out **suicide attacks**
on western targets.

Chief suspect Osama bin Laden, photographed in Afghanistan.

Was there a cause?

Terrorism has been a weapon in Middle East politics since 1948. That year the state of Israel was founded in Palestine, on land claimed by both Jews and Palestinians. Since 1948, Arabs and Israelis have fought four wars. Israel controls most of Palestine.

Children have been drawn into the conflict between the Arabs and Israelis. Palestinian boys gather stones to throw at Israeli soldiers.

Many Palestinians had grown up in **refugee** camps, which became breeding grounds for new generations of terrorists.

Many Arabs supported the Palestinians. They blamed both Israel and the United States for the troubles in their region. Some Arabs also supported Iraq's leader, Saddam Hussein, a leader thought by western countries to be a dangerous **dictator**.

In 1990 Iraq had invaded its small neighbour Kuwait. This had led to the 1991 Gulf War. America and its allies

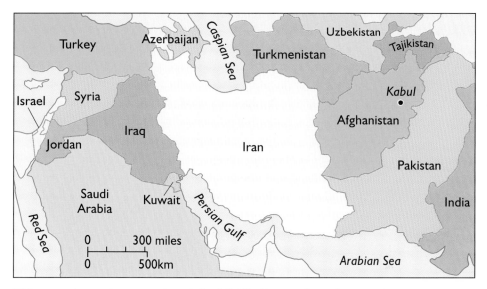

This map shows the countries of the Middle East and south central Asia, where terrorism has played a part in politics since 1948.

had defeated Iraq, but Saddam Hussein was still in power. Some Americans suspected that Saddam Hussein helped terrorists. Others blamed a few Muslim **extremists**, such as al-Qaeda, who hated the west and preached 'holy war' against non-Muslims. Osama bin Laden was believed to be leading a terrorist group based in Afghanistan.

People of all religions, and in almost every country, condemned the 9/11 attacks. Only in Palestine did a few people celebrate a 'victory' for Arab **martyrs** against the west. The Palestinian leader Yasser Arafat expressed his horror at the attack. President Bush now made it clear in a speech: in this new war against terrorism, all nations must choose whose side they were on.

The war in Afghanistan

The US intelligence agencies believed that al-Qaeda was behind the attacks. They began to track down its members within days, as the clearing of the World Trade Center site began. They thought Osama bin Laden was being protected by the Taliban, who ruled Afghanistan.

The Taliban had taken control of Afghanistan in 1996 and had closed it to the outside world. They were strict Muslims, who banned TV and western clothes, ordered men not to shave their beards and stopped girls going to school. The rebels who were fighting the Taliban were not winning. Other Islamic governments feared that the Taliban's style of government might be spread by **revolution** to their own countries.

Taliban fighters in Afghanistan during the civil war in 1995.

The US government asked the Taliban to hand over
Osama bin Laden. When they refused, the US prepared
for war. It sent aid to Afghan rebels, while the US and
its **allies** prepared to remove the Taliban. More than 40
countries, including Britain, France, Germany, Australia
and Russia, helped the United States in various ways.

In October 2001, US, British and other allied forces
attacked Afghanistan. Special forces trekked secretly
into Afghanistan's mountains to hunt the terrorists.
After a short war the Taliban were defeated. A new
government took over in Afghanistan. Some al-Qaeda
terrorists were killed or captured, but there was no
sign of Osama bin Laden.

US warplanes flew from aircraft carriers in the Arabian Sea
to attack targets in Afghanistan.

Choices for America

America had many friends. A French newspaper printed a headline, 'Nous sommes tous Americains' (we are all Americans). At memorial services in America and in other countries, speakers paid moving tributes to the bravery of those who had died. The number of people who had died in the twin towers, which was first estimated to be almost 7,000, was reduced to 2,800 as missing people were discovered alive. One man who had been presumed dead, was found in hospital a year later, suffering from loss of memory.

New York City mayor Rudolph Giuliani attends a memorial service one month after the tragedy.

The world had changed. Many Americans no longer felt as safe as they had previously, even in their own country.

On 7 December 1941, when 2,400 people had been killed at **Pearl Harbor**, America had joined **World War II**.

What would happen after 11 September 2001? On 13 September 2001, President George Bush called the fight against terrorism the 'first war of the 21st century'.

After 9/11 many people were afraid to fly. The US government tightened security at airports. Air travellers could no longer board planes 20 minutes before take-off, with few security checks. US warplanes would shoot down any hijacked airliner thought to pose a danger. A new Department of Homeland Security was set up, to protect Americans at home and co-ordinate the search for terrorists. The hunt for al-Qaeda went on. Greg Michel, a Texas history student, said days after 9/11: 'This is not your typical war. There are no fronts, no trenches.'

Airport security was tightened, to make air travel as safe as possible.

A day of heroism

After 9/11, the world remembered the courage of the people in the hijacked planes, the people in the Pentagon and the twin towers, the firefighters, police and other rescuers. To show they cared, people raised money, sent gifts, even donated shovels, picks and ropes for the rescue work. Father Jordan, a priest in Manhattan, said, 'We have seen evil at its worst, but goodness at its best.'

The events of 9/11 were a very public tragedy. Millions saw and heard what happened through

On 11 September 2002, people lit candles in memory of those who had died on that day the previous year.

mobile phones and live television. In President Bush's words: 'Each of us will remember what happened that day and to whom it happened.'

It took many weeks to clear the World Trade Center site, and get the Pentagon back in shape. The cost, in money as well as in human lives, was high. However, New York City quickly went back to work, hoping that a better world would emerge from the rubble.

New terrorist attacks made headlines: a mysterious **anthrax** attack through the US mail; a theatre siege in Moscow, Russia; a bomb in a nightclub in Bali, Indonesia. Terrorism is hard to defeat. People may have to put up with inconvenience and give up some freedoms to defend themselves against it. Being searched at airports and being watched by spy cameras in shopping centres may be the price of liberty.

New friendships were formed after 9/11. Russia's President Putin became a partner in President Bush's fight against terrorism.

Timeline

1993   Terrorists try to blow up the World Trade Center with a truck bomb in the car park. The explosion causes damage, kills six people and injures more than 1,000.

1995   Japanese terrorists use nerve gas to kill 12 people on the Tokyo subway.

1995   *19 April:* Timothy McVeigh kills 168 people by blowing up an office building in Oklahoma City, USA.

1996   The Taliban seize power in Afghanistan.

1998   *7 August:* al-Qaeda terrorists bomb US embassies in Kenya and Tanzania, killing 224 people. US fires cruise missiles at terrorist bases in Afghanistan and Sudan.

1999   The FBI name Osama bin Laden as 'most wanted terrorist'.

2000   *12 October:* In the port of Aden (Yemen) suicide bombers in a small boat blow a hole in the US Navy ship *Cole*. Seventeen American sailors are killed.

2001   *9 September:* Ahmed Shah Masood, leader of the Northern Alliance rebels in Afghanistan, is assassinated by al-Qaeda suicide bombers posing as journalists.

2001   *11 September:* Three hijacked airliners are used as bombs to attack the World Trade Center and Pentagon buildings in the USA. A fourth hijacked plane crashes.

2001   *12 September:* NATO declares that the 9/11 attack is an attack on its 19-member alliance.

2001	*7 October*: The United States and its allies attack Afghanistan.
2001	*19 October:* US ground troops move into Afghanistan.
2001	*26 October:* President Bush signs a new law, the Anti-Terrorism Act, which gives the US government greater powers to hunt terrorists.
2001	*13 November:* Afghanistan's capital Kabul is captured by coalition forces and Afghan rebels.
2001	*6 December*: The fall of Kandahar, the last Taliban stronghold in Afghanistan.
2001	*22 December:* Richard Reid, a Briton linked to al-Qaeda, is accused of planning to blow up an American airliner with a bomb hidden in his shoe.
2002	*January:* There are reports that Osama bin Laden is dead, but these are not confirmed.
2002	*30 May*: The site of Ground Zero is cleared of the last rubble.
2002	*13 October:* More than 180 people, mostly young tourists, are killed in a car bomb attack on a nightclub in Bali, Indonesia.
2003	*19 February:* Mounir al-Motassadek, the first man to stand trial over the 11 September attacks is jailed for 15 years, found guilty of being an accessory to the murder of more than 3,000 people in the attacks on New York and Washington. The 28-year-old Moroccan was convicted in Germany of being a member of a terrorist organisation and providing back-up to terrorists plotting to hijack planes and fly them into the World Trade Center and the Pentagon.

Glossary

allies Countries who come to the aid of one another in time of war or some other danger.

amputated Cut off by a doctor or medical person; usually this means an arm or leg.

anthrax A dangerous disease which has been tested as a biological weapon.

chief of staff Senior official who works for the US president.

dictator A ruler who rules alone, often harshly.

Eastern Time One of six US time zones.

embassies Buildings housing ambassadors and their staff, who represent their country in foreign countries.

employees People who are employed by (work for) a company.

evacuate To leave a building in danger.

extremists People with extreme views and a belief in their own rightness, usually unwilling to listen to other opinions.

FBI The Federal Bureau of Investigation, the national crime-fighting agency of the US Department of Justice.

hijacker A person who takes over a plane during a flight.

jet fuel The oil-based fuel burned by jet engines.

martyr Someone who dies for their religious beliefs.

Muslim A follower of the religion of Islam.

NATO The North Atlantic Treaty Organisation, 19 nations in Europe and North America.

newscasters TV presenters of news programmes.

peace process A series of talks and agreements aimed at ending a dispute.

Pearl Harbor A US naval base in Hawaii, attacked by Japanese naval planes in 1941.

refugee Someone who is made homeless by war and unable to return home.

revolution The violent overthrow of one system to set up another.

Secretary of State The member of the US government in charge of foreign policy – dealings with other countries.

skyscraper A very tall building with many floors.

sprinkler system A safety system in buildings which sprays water on to a fire.

State Department The US government department for foreign affairs, headed by the Secretary of State.

suicide attacks Attacks, often with bombs, made by people who know they too will die.

squeegee A tool with a rubber-covered blade, used for cleaning windows.

terrorist Someone who carries out violent acts for political ends, often against civilian targets.

truck-bomb A truck filled with explosives, either parked close to a target or driven at it.

White House The Washington home of the President of the United States.

World War II The war fought from 1939-45 between the Axis powers (Germany, Italy, Japan) and the Allies (Britain, Russia, the United States and others).

Index

September 2001 11 September